Tropical Flowers

Tropical Flowers

EILEEN W. JOHNSON

FLORAL DESIGNS BY **FELIPE SASTRE**

PHOTOGRAPHS BY **ADRIAN MUELLER**

GIBBS SMITH
TO ENRICH AND INSPIRE HUMANKIND

First Edition
16 15 14 13 12   5 4 3 2 1

Published by
Gibbs Smith
P.O. Box 667
Layton, Utah 84041

1.800.835.4993 orders
www.gibbs-smith.com

Cover and Book Design by Michelle Farinella Design
Printed and bound in China
Gibbs Smith books are printed on either recycled, 100% post-consumer waste, FSC-certified papers or on paper produced from sustainable PEFC-certified forest/controlled wood source. Learn more at www.pefc.org.

Library of Congress Cataloging-in-Publication Data

Johnson, Eileen W.
Tropical flowers / Eileen W. Johnson ; floral arrangements by Felipe
Sastre ; photographs by Adrian Mueller. -- 1st ed.
    p. cm.
ISBN 978-1-4236-2420-2
1. Flower arrangement. 2. Tropical plants. I. Title.
SB449.3.T76J64 2012
635.9'66--dc23
                              2012012136

To my father who gave me unquestioned love and taught me

the value of integrity in all things great and small.

Contents

Acknowledgments

I would like to thank the many friends and colleagues who helped me put together this book as well as those who put up with me while I wrote the text. First and foremost, thank you to Adrian Mueller whose beautiful photographs made it all possible, and to Felipe Sastre for allowing me to put his vision of tropical flowers into a book. Thanks also go to Angelika Frantzen for the use of her apartment on Washington Square, to Cheryl Hill for her patience and loyalty during the writing of this and other books, Michael Pochna for his friendship and kindness, to Maria Theresa Mata, to Cornelia Guest for allowing us to photograph the greenhouses at her Old Westbury estate, Caribbean Cuts for their magnificent tropical flowers and leaves, Gary Page for his selection of orchids from all over the world, and the New York Botanical Gardens for their expansive library which was so helpful in my research. In our bridal chapter, I would like to thank Jennifer Aviles for her modeling of the bridal gowns, John James for his hair styling and Marie-Josee Lafontaine for her makeup styling. The bridal gowns were graciously lent to us from I Do... I Do... Bridal in Morristown, New Jersey.

Introduction

For many people, tropical flowers are often whimsical, seductive and alien creatures. Some of them look more like insects or tiny animals. Brightly colored and oddly shaped, they just don't seem to behave like cultivated roses or hydrangeas. Are they modern or otherworldly? How do they work in contemporary environments of glass and steel?

Orchids have long been associated with obsessive collectors, hidden fortunes and erudite amateur botanists. New species are still being discovered and named while at the same time we can find numerous varieties for sale at local supermarkets. I have long been intrigued by their beauty and mystery. For me and for many of the florists whom I work with at FlowerSchool New York, tropical flowers have always been the exotic "other."

Through working with a talented florist like Felipe Sastre, I have learned a great deal about the subject. Felipe not only knows how to design with tropical flowers, but he also grew up with them. They are a part of his culture, and his vocabulary, so to speak.

What I have learned in researching this book is more than how to use elephant ears as place mats or how to make a minimalist look with ginger or anthurium. I have a new respect for the vibrant colors of the tropics and a love for the varying colors of greens.

The exotic realm of orchids was characterized by Samuel Beckett who said of the preening aristocratic characters in Proust's *Remembrance of Things Past* ". . . they are shameless, exposing their genitals." Indeed, orchids were given their name by Theophrastus, a Greek philosopher who lived between 370 and 285 B.C. He called them "orkhis"(the Greek word for testicles) because the plant

had two tubers in the shape of an olive. Orchids have always seemed seductive. Once again talking of Proust, Swann and his great love Odette called lovemaking "doing the cattleya" as a reference to the sweet-smelling cattleya orchid that Odette wore the first time they embraced.

I've learned much about the history of tropical flowers in the west, some of it not so pretty or flattering to Europeans. Many of us think of the *Mutiny on the Bounty* as a great adventure movie and book, but how many of us know that the *Bounty*'s mission was to go to the islands in the Pacific in order to bring breadfruit to the Caribbean, where it was to be harvested as food for the recently arrived slaves from Africa?

We now live in a society in which exotic fruits, plants and flowers travel the world packed in cargo holds of supersonic jets, where they are readily available to the average consumer in Saint Petersburg, Anchorage, or New York. We can easily forget that there was a time "plant hunters" risked their lives and fortunes to transport them.

No longer can I look at a magnificent Bird of Paradise flower without thinking that its Latin name is *Strelitzia Reginae*, named after Princess Charlotte of Mecklenburg-Strelitz, an amateur botanist and a patroness of Mozart, who was married to George the Third of England.

I want you, the reader, to understand the unique beauty of these flowers as well as their continuing ability to be adapted to the modern environment that we live in. They have in all their beauty and oddness completely seduced me and become my new passion. I can only hope that this book will instill that passion in many more people in the years to come.

Phalaenopsis javanica are hybridized orchids originally from the island of Java in Indonesia. Many orchid fanciers around the world grow them; however, most are commercially produced in Southeast Asia. Phalaenopsis orchids were very popular among Victorian collectors and are among the most popular orchid plants sold today.

1

Greenhouses
and
Orangeries

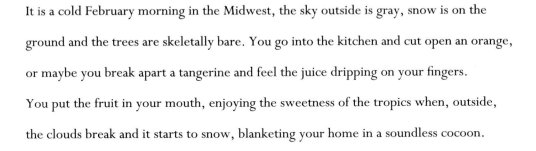

It is a cold February morning in the Midwest, the sky outside is gray, snow is on the ground and the trees are skeletally bare. You go into the kitchen and cut open an orange, or maybe you break apart a tangerine and feel the juice dripping on your fingers. You put the fruit in your mouth, enjoying the sweetness of the tropics when, outside, the clouds break and it starts to snow, blanketing your home in a soundless cocoon.

We now take these things for granted in the northern hemisphere, having our sweet morsel of fresh citrus in the middle of a long winter. But for many centuries, these tastes were the purview of the richest of the rich. To have an orange in the middle of winter in the seventeenth century meant that you had to have an orangery in your castle. A winter garden had to be built and kept heated. Orange trees had to be transported from the "new world" of the tropics by ship over periods of months to years.

The oldest greenhouse in Europe that is still in existence is in Padua, Italy, and is a World Heritage Site of UNESCO. It was created in 1545 in order to develop and propagate plants from around the world to be used for medicinal properties. The greenhouse's website reads: "The Botanical Garden of Padova is the original of all botanical gardens throughout the world; it represents the birth of science, of scientific exchanges, and of the awareness of the relationship between nature and culture. It gave

Spider orchids——are they insects or animals?
It is difficult to tell.

a great contribution to the development of many modern scientific disciplines, notably botany, medicine, chemistry, ecology, and pharmacy."

The gardens of the Sun King, Louis XIV, were built many years later. They, too, were started for medicinal purposes and evolved into botanical gardens that showcased the breadth and wealth of the French empire.

The greenhouses at Planting Fields Arboretum in Oyster Bay, Long Island, are among the largest and best kept winter gardens in the United States.

Cornelia Guest whose home in Old Westbury has its landscape designed by the great Russell Page has graciously offered us a look at her exceptional private greenhouses in which lemon and orange trees thrive among orchids and other exotic plants.

These orchids are grown commercially
in a heated greenhouse on eastern
Long Island. Rows upon rows grow
underneath artificial lighting that
mimics their tropical habitats.

Facing and left: Exotic plants such as these giant palms inside a forty-foot-tall arboretum were originally transported from the tropics on large ships. Explorers raced each other to find newer and rarer varieties.

A small tropical plant such as this kumquat inside a house would enliven the bleakest of winters.

The orchid greenhouse of Cornelia Guest is part of one of the remaining private estates on Long Island. At the time we took this photograph, the orchids had just been transported from the area around the pool to the greenhouse, where they will spend autumn, winter and spring. The hot, humid summers of Long Island can make these blooms thrive; however, once the cold sets in, they need protection. Guest has several greenhouses on her estate containing orange trees and lemon trees, among other plants. This is one of the last of the private greenhouses in the area. Heating costs in winter as well as difficulty with finding people who understand how to care for tropical plants has made tropical greenhouses almost extinct.

Facing: Lemon trees originated in Asia and were most likely introduced to Europe in the first century during the time of Ancient Rome.

Left: These citrus trees have a good home in this greenhouse that was built many years ago.

Facing: The intricate details of this flowering aloe plant are stunning.

Left: Planting Fields Arboretum on the North Shore of Long Island is home to this large greenhouse. Once a gold coast private mansion, the property is now a New York State Park and is open to visitors much of the year.

ORANGERIES

From the 1700s to the 1900s, orangeries were built throughout Europe from Italy to Moscow to Paris to Stockholm as a display of wealth and status. An orangery was a type of greenhouse made of glass and built on the grounds of a wealthy person's residence primarily to grow citrus fruit during the long and harsh winters of Europe. Other shrubs, exotic plants and orchids were also grown in orangeries. Stoves were often used to keep the buildings heated. Today, many of the grand estates no longer can afford the upkeep with the price of electricity being so high. Old Westbury Gardens, one of the largest estates on the North Shore of Long Island, no longer keeps its palmerie (a greenhouse exclusively dedicated to palms) heated during the winter because of the expense.

A Dutch Masterpiece *in* Flowers

When one thinks of tropical flowers, one rarely thinks in terms of Dutch Masterpiece paintings. The paintings of the Dutch masters usually featured tulips, roses, hydrangeas, ranunculus and fritillaria.

In this first arrangement, Felipe has re-created a Dutch still life using only tropical flowers and leaves. It would be perfectly at home in a contemporary apartment as well as a traditional home. The colors are bright—brighter than most still lifes. The lines are linear. There is a grace and flow to the design that suggests a natural elegance.

To put together this arrangement, Felipe used a variety of tropical flowers and berries as well as palms. This requires a sharp knife. We use a standard florist's knife at FlowerSchool New York, a large clear glass vase and some floral tape. The tropical ingredients are:

Bonita bromeliads

Hanging heliconias or rostrata

'Prince of Darkness' heliconias

Schefflera berries

Hala fronds

First, the bonita bromeliad is stripped by hand rather than by knife.

Felipe cuts the bonita bromeliad with the florist's knife. Notice the position of his hand while he cuts the stem.

Facing: Tropical leaves show the many colors of green when exposed to sunlight.

Left: Next, we'll prepare the hanging heliconias, which will add another dimension of texture and color to the floral arrangement. These tropical beauties can grow up to fifteen feet in length.

Right and facing: The heliconia stems are wrapped in moist cotton so that they are kept hydrated during the long journey from the tropics. Notice how Felipe cuts the stems at an angle so they can absorb an adequate amount of water and last longer.

Felipe makes a cut in the stem of the hanging heliconia. The plant's main pollinators are hummingbirds.

The outer part of the stem is
carefully removed and discarded.

The next step in making this
arrangement is to clean the schefflera
berries off their woody branches so
that none of the berries are beneath
the water line of the vase. To do this,
Felipe holds the stem in one hand and
flicks off the berries with the knife
using the other hand.

Make sure to use a sharp florist's knife when removing the berries from the stems.

Right and facing: Schefflera trees are also called octopus trees or umbrella trees and are native to New Guinea, Australia and Java. The berries and subsequent flowers sprout at the top of the trees like a mad scientist's wild hair.

Right and facing: Felipe slices the hala frond down the middle. The hala tree is native to Hawaii and the leaves have been put to many uses by Hawaiians over the years, including weaving them into materials for roofs. The sweet-smelling pollen of the male flowers has been used to preserve the flowers of traditional Hawaiian leis.

Felipe cuts the end of the hala frond. He uses a product called Sure-Stik made by Floralife to tape the frond together.

He tapes the two ends together so they form a circle, and the stem of the leaf is left long so that it will rest in the vase.

Right and facing: Felipe finishes taping the hala leaf. When creating this floral arrangement, you can decide if you prefer tighter or looser circles.

The hala fronds are now ready to

be placed in the arrangement.

To build the arrangement in a vase, the bonita bromeliad stems are placed in a crisscross pattern so that they create a base for the other stems to rest on. The hanging heliconias are added next in a crisscross pattern.

Facing: Felipe places the 'Prince of Darkness' heliconias between the hanging heliconias.

Left: The schefflera berries are the last element before the ornamental hala fronds.

In this arrangement, the stems
have become a part of the design,
as everything is clean, clear
and graphic.

A TROPICAL STILL LIFE

Many of the Dutch still lifes in the Rijksmuseum in Amsterdam

are painted with a dark, almost black background, so we thought

it might be interesting to show tropical flowers in the same vein.

This arrangement is reminiscent of an Abraham Mignon still life

from the middle of the seventeenth century, the way the reds of the

hanging heliconias dominate the other colors. Felipe feels that in

the rainforest the bright colors of the hanging heliconias are a shiny

contrast to the greens of the other plants.

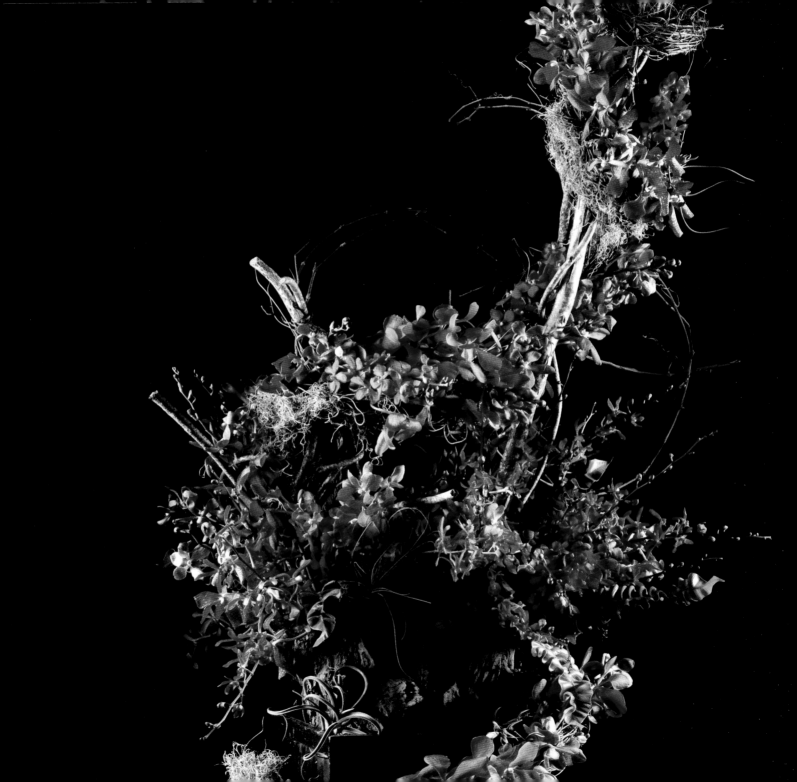

3

A Modern Interpretation *of* Orchids

Orchids, though not limited to the tropics (orchids are native to every continent except Antarctica), are looked upon by many as the ne plus ultra of tropical flowers. It is estimated that there may be as many as 25,000 orchid species.

In this unique arrangement, Felipe uses mokara and dendrobium orchids. The mokara is a hybrid orchid made of arachnis, asocentrum and vanda orchids. It was created in 1969 in Singapore. The dendrobium was named by a Swedish botanist in 1799 who combined the two words "dendros," or tree, and "bios," or life, which together formed the name "dendrobium." Translated, dendrobium means plants that grow on trees, a perfect description of an epiphyte, or what we call an air plant.

This design was originally used as a centerpiece for the New York Botanical Gardens' annual Orchid Dinner, which helps raise funds for its vital research. Using oasis (floral foam), hollowed-out roots and large vines, the sculptural look mimics the way these flowers bloom in their native environments. Many of us are used to seeing orchids as plants. We do not realize that their natural habitat is usually high in the air.

First, the block of oasis needs to be soaked in clean, cold water before it is cut. The oasis is used to construct the base of the arrangement.

Using a sharp knife, Felipe cuts the
oasis to fit into the hollowed root.

The vines are secured in the oasis in order to create a solid base.

Here, Felipe surrounds the oasis with damp Spanish moss so that the oasis is no longer visible.

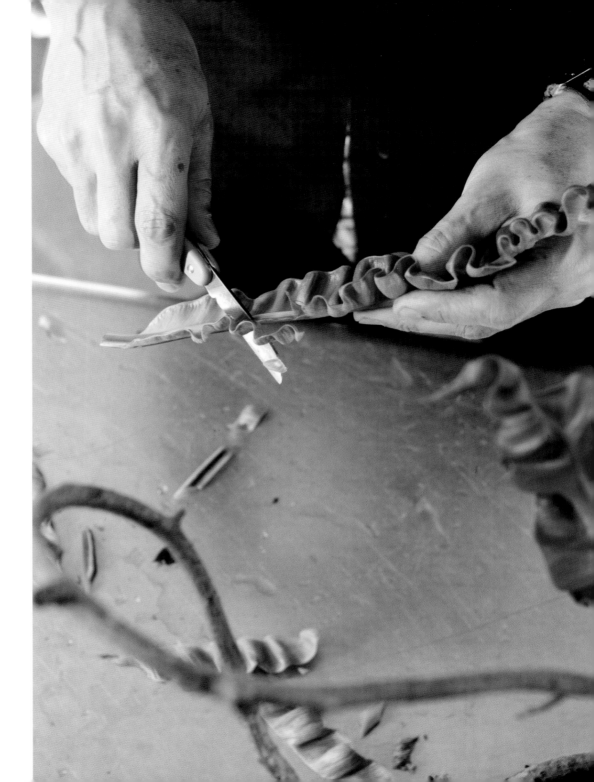

The bottom of the leaf is cut so that it will be sharp enough to go through the oasis.

The wire pictured is called vine wire. When used with grape vines, it becomes invisible. When designing constructions such as this, it is important that the mechanics not be visible.

Right: The leaf is placed firmly in the oasis using the knife-sharpened point.

Facing: Felipe twists the vines and makes them look like they are celestial orbs.

Right: The structure is made so that the orchids can be seen to grow in the air. Indeed, these orchids are epiphytic, which means they grow on trees and depend on moisture and nutrients from the air. Many orchids are epiphytic.

Facing: Felipe twists the vine wire so that it becomes a part of the structure.

*Next, the stems of the orchids
should be placed in water tubes.
In order for the stems to fit
into the tubes, they should be
narrowed with a florist's knife.*

Water tubes will help to keep the arrangement from drying out. This way, the arrangement will last for several days.

Facing: Natural angel vine hair is used to create a bird's nest look. It can be sourced from a crafts store.

Left: Here, Felipe fits the orchids into the root.

Facing and left: Felipe uses Spanish moss to cover the water tube. Spanish moss is not really a moss even though most people call it that. It is an epiphyte. Off a tree and refrigerated, Spanish moss can stay fresh for many weeks.

Right: Felipe's finished creation is surrounded by air plants at the base.

Facing: This close-up shows beautiful shapes and patterns on the petals of the mokaras.

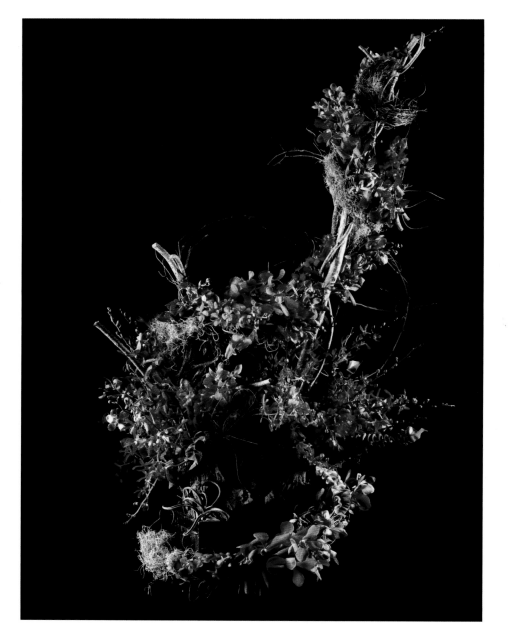

A genus of dendrobium orchids
is used in traditional Chinese
medicine. The are 1,800 genera of
this orchid, including a 'Margaret
Thatcher' dendrobium cultivated
at the National Orchid Garden in
Singapore.

AN ORCHID DELIGHT

For Felipe, this floral arrangement reminded him of a tree trunk that

he had seen invaded by orchids, air plants and vines—almost taken

over by those elements. Many people think of air plants as parasites,

which is not the case. They grow on trees but get their nutrients

from the air and water, not from their host.

4

The Mermaid *Bride*

This bride wanted a look that was inspired by Shakespeare's *A Midsummer Night's Dream*. What could be more appropriate than tropical flowers that look as if they came from the sea? In much of the tropics, the sea is in close proximity, so we devised several arrangements for our bride that made her look like Prospero's daughter, Miranda, getting married.

Strands of rhipsalis, an epiphytic plant most commonly found in Central American rainforests, are entwined with Spanish moss. Phalaenopsis and stephanotis orchids are delicately wired onto the rhipsalis, making it look as if our bride is encircled with magical seaweed. Rhipsalis is related to mistletoe, which is also an airborne plant.

A phalaenopsis orchid encircles the
bride's wrist.

The bride's hair is also adorned with phalaenopsis orchids.

Right: This style of layering orchids is perfect for a bride with long, thick hair.

Facing: Long, flowing bridal bouquets have recently become fashionable again. This bouquet contains just three elements——rhipsalis, Spanish moss and phalaenopsis orchids——and is as light to hold as it is to look at.

Our bride is carrying a tight bouquet of curcuma flowers wrapped with rhipsalis. The rhipsalis is malleable, making it a perfect covering for the stems of the curcuma flowers.

It is hard to believe that these curcuma flowers are tropical unless you were raised in the tropics. Originally from Southeast Asia, they have the delicate look of a tulip crossed with a rose. They are in the ginger family and their roots are used to make turmeric, a spice that is well known in cooking and is considered to have valuable medicinal properties. Recent studies have credited turmeric with everything from being an antiseptic to curing arthritis and cancer.

Facing: These curcuma flowers wrapped in rhipsalis look like an offering from the sea.

Left: The front of our bride, Jennifer Aviles, is decorated with a lei made of orchids. Leis can be purchased at a wholesale florist or made by stringing dendrobium orchids together with thin wires.

This time the bride has stephanotis
orchids wired into her hair. The
blossoms have a distinctly sweet
smell that many great perfumers try
to capture.

Felipe has fashioned a ring out of a large rust-colored cymbidium orchid and a piece of black ribbon.

Facing: A more autumnal look is achieved with a cascading bouquet made of rust-colored cymbidium orchids, rhipsalis strands, sea grapes and brown grosgrain ribbon.

Left: A close-up of the bouquet, focusing on the sea grapes, or Coccoloba uvifera, *a small evergreen plant that is found in seacoasts of tropical regions. Resistant to sand and wind, these plants are cultivated to provide barriers in beach regions. The sea grapes can be used to make jam as well.*

A gardenia is placed delicately in the
bride's hair. The cultivation of these
scented flowers goes back more than a
thousand years to the Sung Dynasty
of China. The flowers were depicted
in paintings and on porcelains most
prominently during the Ming Dynasty
and first propagated in England
during the mid-eighteenth century.
Gardenias are delicate and bruise
easily. Fashion designer Tom Ford
always sets aside an extra gardenia to
wear on his lapel during special events
so that if the gardenia he is wearing
turns brown, it can be easily changed
for a pure white one. The fragrance of
a gardenia is so strong that floating
one in a bowl of water at bedside can
scent an entire house.

MERMAID FANTASY

We call our bride the Mermaid Bride because her look is of someone raised by the sea, as many tropical flowers are. We wanted to create a look that was other-worldly and referenced Shakespeare's *The Tempest*. It is hard to imagine that Shakespeare would have created a fantasy like *The Tempest* without the explorers and exotic plant-hunters who navigated the waters of the Caribbean in search of treasures. Mermaids were the exotic "other" that many people associate with the tropics today. They are a part of the mythology that draws many people from northern climes to leave their lives behind them and start anew in the tropics.

5

A Tropical Lunch *in* *the* Sky

For this luncheon party, Felipe has used green as the main color. As colorful as the tropics often are, the color green always predominates. How it must have surprised the explorers from Europe who first saw the vibrant greens of the tropics where trees and bushes stayed green year-round and flowers masqueraded as insects, fruits and animals!

The mixture of art and furniture in the apartment is quite representative of the modern world of the tropics today. There is a deep appreciation of the products of the land, a desire to return to nature while acknowledging the European roots that have been established over the past centuries. While there is much pain in this history, there is much to celebrate—the family that lives in this apartment has created an environment that has managed to combine these diverse elements with grace.

The table is laden with some of the treasures of the tropics including bamboo stalks, sea grapes, green anthuriums and coconuts. The explorers named anthuriums after the Greek word for fruit, "anthos," and the Greek word for tail, "ouros."

Above and facing: Elephant ears, more correctly called philodendron leaves, lie underneath the arrangement. They can be used as place mats, but in this setting Felipe has chosen Pacific fan palms for use under the plates. The dishes are from Siena, Italy, home of the famous Palio, a horse race through the streets of the ancient city that dates back to the sixteenth century. The water goblets are Venetian.

Green anthuriums paired with bamboo are a

lovely combination for a tropical tablescape.

The eighteenth-century Venetian
table is laden with many of the
spoils of the tropics: coconuts,
green anthuriums, bamboo stalks
and sea grapes. In the background
are pictures of the conquistadors,
a reminder of the Spanish and
Portuguese who made their marks on
the American tropics.

Sunlight gracefully peeks through
Dracaena marginata *cuttings and*
envelops yellow anthuriums.

Yellow anthuriums, red ginger and
Dracaena marginata *make an airy*
arrangement and are particularly
interesting placed in a vase next to
ancient Greek sculptures.

Right: Another easy-to-make, simple arrangement that should last up to two weeks is this combination of cuttings from a Dracaena marginata, *which has its origins in Madagascar, and a few Pacific fan tail palms. Once again, a clear glass cylinder is used as a vase that is lined with a croton leaf.*

Facing: A simple arrangement of pincushion protea (native to South Africa) and red ginger in a cylinder vase lined with a calathea leaf. An arrangement such as this is easy to make and quite hardy with both the ginger and the pincushion protea lasting up to two weeks.

6

Dinner
above
Manhattan

When we first set the table for this festive dinner, the husband of the hostess looked in and exclaimed, "It feels like I am sitting down to a dinner in the rainforest!" We were in the middle of Manhattan, fifty stories high. So high up that it seemed as if we were on the same level as the helicopters observing the traffic below. This is the magic of New York; you can re-create the atmosphere of distant lands by merely shopping in the right places. Our destination was a wholesaler called Caribbean Cuts on West 28th Street. There, we were able to buy all the elements involved in the tropical tablescape that replicated the feeling of a rainforest high above the canyons of modern skyscrapers.

The formal dining table is set with Herend China. Instead of using formal place mats, Felipe put monstera leaves under the green service plates. All the elements together—the pinks of the pepperberries, the yellows of the rattlesnake calathea, the browns of the chocolate bananas, and the reds of the James Story orchids against the greens of the various tropical flowers make the center of the dinner table look like an exotic tropical still life.

Facing: The centerpiece of the table is a large stalk of chocolate bananas. Felipe is replicating the feeling of warmth that he had when visiting his grandmother's house near Veracruz in which she always had a stalk of bananas hanging in front of the stove. This she did so that they would become yellow faster. Bougainvillea, mango trees, gardenia and jasmine surrounded her home. These scents are strong, and would not have been appropriate to place in the center of a dining table, so Felipe used texture and color as a metaphor for the sultry and sweet scents rather than using the flowers themselves.

Left: A multicolored croton leaf serves as a beautiful backing for this place card. Croton leaves, like many tropical leaves, are both malleable and substantial, so they can be used in a variety of ways. They are often used to line clear glass vases since they tend not to create as much bacteria as other leaves.

The owner of the apartment is a collector of art and artifacts from many different regions. These sculptural lights are made of gourds from Africa by Nicolas Cesbron, a French artist who works with wood from Africa and the Americas. The juxtaposition of the tropical leaves and orchids in the vase against the gourds and lights of the cityscape add a dimension of interplay that is almost magical.

The simplest arrangement of thirty stems of dendrobium orchids in a mason jar are quite striking. Dendrobium orchids, once exotic and expensive, have become quite common in flower shops and grocery stores. Some of them are dyed in frightening, unnatural colors. These yellow ones have been hybridized. They require very little skill to arrange and are inexpensive and long lasting.

The entrance table has a silver tray with a Herend tea service surrounded by fish tail palms, known as "Whoopi Goldbergs" by the wholesaler. In the tall vase, yellow and red dendrobium orchids add a splendid dash of color. Votive lights highlight the dreadlock-like fish tail palms. Set on top of the burnished nineteenth-century table from France with the Hungarian china, the tablescape Felipe has created is a melding of the old European world and the tropical flora of the new world of the Americas.

COCONUTS

In the tropics, coconuts are a part of the daily diet for many people.

Coconut oil and milk are used in cooking, cosmetics and soap.

In Malaysia, monkeys are used to harvest the coconuts from the

tops of the palm trees. Competitions are held each year in order

to determine the fastest of these pig-tailed macaques. Worldwide,

coconuts are cultivated in more than eighty countries, with the

Philippines leading in production.

7

On Washington Square *with* Bromeliads *and* Palms

Some of the most popular plants being used today are bromeliads, a plant family known most commonly as air plants. These plants are members of a family of more than 3,000 types called Bromeliaceae. They include Spanish moss and pineapples. Some of them are indeed air plants, which means that they get their nutrition from the air and water and live high on trees. Others can be terrestrial, meaning that they grow in the earth like other plants. What they all have in common are scales that absorb nutrition and water. They are strong and tenacious. They are so popular that there is even a society called the Bromeliad Society International (www.bsi.org).

We decided to show an arrangement of bromeliads in a town house apartment on Washington Square that is said to be the setting for Henry James' novella of the same name. This is a particularly appropriate venue since bromeliads were once the choice of wealthy collectors with greenhouses or winter gardens. Both palms and bromeliads would have been used as original elements of décor in this 1880's home.

Bromeliads have become popular in today's design world for a variety of reasons. They last for long periods of time without water, which makes them quite practical. They provide unusual textures and their flowers have colors that are almost psychedelic.

The first bromeliad in the European world was a pineapple that Columbus brought back to Spain on his second voyage to the West Indies in 1493. It is hard to imagine how sweet its succulent fruit must have tasted at the Spanish court in the fifteenth century!

Felipe stands in front of the bromeliads that he will use in his arrangement. As you can see, bromeliads come in a variety of shapes and sizes.

Author Eileen Johnson and floral designer Felipe Sastre stand in the Washington Square apartment of Angelika Frantzen.

This rhipsalis, a bromeliad,
also known as mistletoe cactus,
hangs from trees in abundance in
Veracruz, Mexico, where Felipe
grew up. While mistletoe is often
a scarce and precious commodity
in Northern America, it grows in
profusion in tropical rainforests.
Here, Felipe ties it with green
florist's wire so that it will form
a circle.

The rhipsalis will serve as a cushion under a shell that will be placed on the next level of this floral design.

Right and facing: A hollowed shell from a palm fruit is used as a natural container. In the tropics, palm fruits are used to make a variety of different foods, from palm oil to coconut milk to dates. Currently, in many tropical areas, palm fruits are being used to make biofuel, which has led to the destruction of the tropical rainforest in countries such as Malaysia and Thailand. Felipe cushions the rhipsalis around the shell and then adds the first bromeliad plant.

Right and facing: More bromeliads are added. They are simply placed in the palm fruit shell container— no water or dirt is needed. This is as simple as flower arranging gets.

Facing and left: The bromeliads are placed in the container without using wire or tape. There is no need for water as they will look good for several weeks taking nourishment from the air.

The final arrangement has two large bromeliads anchoring it. This display will last for several weeks with an occasional misting.

Elephant ears and fish tail palms against a rubber tree create drama in a corner of the dining room.

A simple but graphic display using two giant philodendron leaves with palms in a clear glass vase is elegantly highlighted on the family's grand piano.

BROMELIADS

Bromeliads have been used for food and fiber as well as religious

ceremonies for thousands of years by the ancient Aztecs and Incas.

The pineapple, first brought to Europe by Christopher Columbus,

is among the largest of the bromeliads. Spanish moss is the smallest.

The stems of pineapples are used as a primary ingredient for

meat tenderizers.

Tropical
Christmas

It is Christmas morning and our family is in New York City—not in the tropics, basking in the sun. To celebrate a cross-cultural Christmas, a Frazer Fir Christmas tree was purchased from Vermont and decorated with that most typical of tropical flowers, ginger.

The history of ginger goes back more than 5,000 years, when it was first recorded that the Chinese used its root for medicinal purposes. The ancient Romans, who brought it from India, also used it medicinally. Queen Elizabeth I is credited with using precious ginger spice from the East in making the first gingerbread men for Christmas. Ginger has been an important factor in the spice trade for many centuries and has been quite expensive in the past. It reached the New World via the Spanish conquistadors in the middle of the sixteenth century.

Felipe remembers it growing by the side of the road outside Veracruz, where its long red heads stuck out like roosters' crowns growing on long stalks in the fields. To use ginger flowers as decorations for Christmas, soak the flowers in water before wiring them to the evergreen branches. This is important since they do not drink water through their stems but through their flowers. This could make for a spectacular, if not long-lasting, Christmas ornament. At least fifty ginger flowers would be needed for a six-foot evergreen.

Facing: The bright color and ornamental design of ginger flowers make them perfect for using as holiday decorations.

Left: A fire in the fireplace creates a warm ambiance. The temple illustration above the mantel is from India, where ginger is used to spice foods on an everyday basis. Although many tropical countries now grow ginger, China and India are still the main exporters.

The fireplace mantel has a base of boxwood and then is ornamented by tropical plants including sea grapes, James Story orchids and fish tail palm.

This cluster of ginger flowers on a bed of fish tail palm is probably the simplest tropical arrangement you can make for a table centerpiece. Once again, quantity is important. Use at least thirty ginger flowers to create a look of abundance.

CYMBIDIUM ORCHIDS

Cymbidium orchids are one of the most popular varieties of orchids

sold in the United States. The name is from the Greek "kymbes,"

meaning boat shaped. Cymbidiums are native to Korea, Japan,

China, Australia and Southeast Asia. We know that they have been

cultivated in China for more than 2,500 years. A large stem of

cymbidium orchids can have as many as twenty blossoms. These

blossoms can be pulled off the stem and put in small containers. They

make great little decorative statements in small areas of the home

such as in bathrooms, guestrooms and hallways.

Resources

American Institute of Floral Designers (AIFD)

aifd.org

The Boston Flower Exchange

thebostonflowerexchange.com

The Botanical Garden in Padova

A UNESCO World Heritage Site, it is the oldest academic garden in its original site.

ortobotanico.unipd.it/en/index.html

Caribbean Cuts

This wholesaler specializes in leaves and flowers imported directly from their farms in the Caribbean. It also has an excellent website for the identification of tropicals.

caribbeancuts.com

Florist's Review

floristsreview.com

Flower

This magazine is dedicated to "enriching life through flowers."

flowermag.com

Foliage Gardens

This is New York's premier location for purchasing tropical plants. All plants are grown in vast indoor greenhouses on eastern Long Island.

foliagegardens.com

G Page

One of New York's leading flower wholesalers, G Page has an extensive selection of cut orchids for sale.

gpage.com

Los Angeles Flower District Association

laflowerdistrict.com

New York Botanical Gardens

One of the leading botanical garden's in the world, the New York Botanical Gardens is home to many tropical plants and flowers. Home of the yearly "Orchid Show" the New York Botanical Gardens is a leading home of research, sustainability and education.

nybg.org

Royal Botanic Gardens, Kew

First and foremost a scientific organization, with collections of plants, plant products and botanical information.

kew.org

San Francisco Flower Mart

sfflmart.com

Society of American Florists

safnow.org

Wholesale Florist & Floral Supplier Association

wffsa.org